Sports Illustrated KIDS

# BASEBALL'S
# BEST AND WORST

## A Guide to the Game's Good, Bad, and Ugly

by

DREW LYON

CAPSTONE PRESS
a capstone imprint

Sports Illustrated Kids The Best and Worst of Sports are published by
Capstone Press 1710 Roe Crest Drive, North Mankato, Minnesota 56003
www.mycapstone.com

**Cataloging-in-Publication Data**
Names: Lyon, Drew, author.
Title: Baseball's best and worst : a guide to the game's good, bad, and ugly
  / by Drew Lyon.
Description: North Mankato, Minnesota : Capstone Press, 2018. | Series:
  Sports illustrated kids. The best and worst of sports | Audience: Age  9-14.
Identifiers: LCCN 2017047198 (print) | LCCN 2017048693 (ebook) |
ISBN 9781543506211 (eBook PDF) | ISBN 9781543506136 (hardcover)
Subjects:  LCSH: Baseball—Miscellanea—Juvenile literature.
Classification: LCC GV867.5 (ebook) | LCC GV867.5 .L86 2018 (print) | DDC
  796.357—dc23
LC record available at https://lccn.loc.gov/2017047198

**Editorial Credits**
Nate LeBoutillier, editor; Bob Lentz and Terri Poburka, designers;
Eric Gohl, media researcher; Laura Manthe, production specialist

**Photo Credits**
AP Photo: 7 (bottom), 10; Getty Images: Focus on Sport, 20 (bottom), 25 (right),
George Gojkovich, 21, Icon Sportswire, 27 (bottom), Ron Kuntz Collection,
11 (top); Library of Congress: 6; Newscom: Ai Wire/Jorge Lemus, 4–5, AI Wire
Photo Service/Mike Yelman, 25 (left), Cal Sport Media/Kyle Rivas, 9 (bottom),
Everett Collection, 29 (bottom left), Icon Sportswire/Frank Jansky, 15 (top), Icon
Sportswire/Leslie Plaza Johnson, cover (left), Icon Sportswire/Mark LoMoglio, 7
(top), UPI/Bill Greenblatt, 26, UPI/Brian Kersey, 9 (top), UPI/Kamil Krzaczynski,
15 (bottom), ZUMA Press/Dick Druckman, 14; Sports Illustrated: Al Tielemans,
cover (right), 19 (top), 22 (bottom), Chuck Solomon, 17, 24 (right), Damian
Strohmeyer, 12, 13 (bottom), David E. Klutho, 23 (bottom), Heinz Kluetmeier,
28 (top),29 (top left), John Biever, 11 (bottom), 13 (top), 22 (top), John Iacono,
16 (all), John W. McDonough, 20 (top), 27 (top), Lane Stewart, 23 (top), Mark
Kauffman, 29 (top right), Robert Beck, 8, 19 (bottom), Simon Bruty, 18, 28
(bottom), Tony Triolo, 24 (left)

Printed and bound in the United States of America.
010783S18

# TABLE of CONTENTS

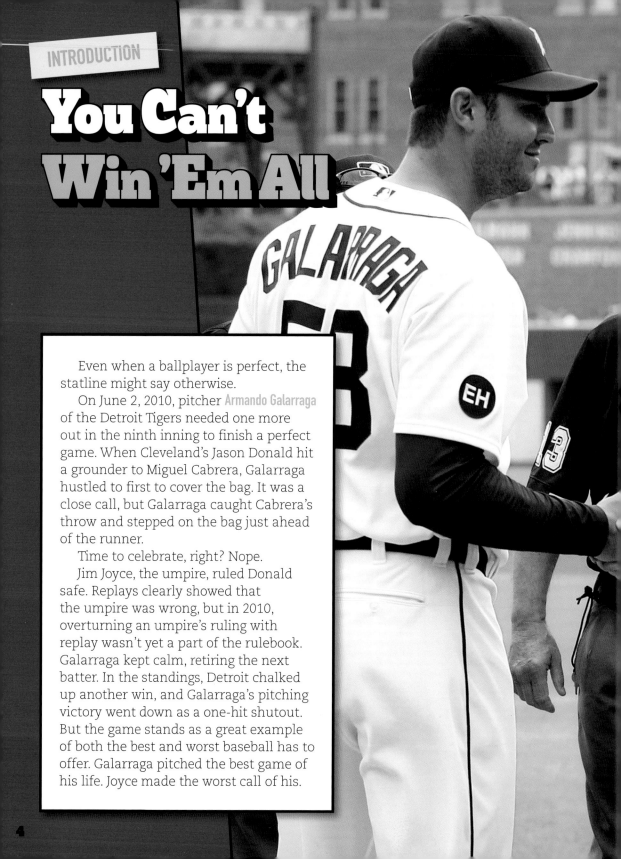

# You Can't Win 'Em All

Even when a ballplayer is perfect, the statline might say otherwise.

On June 2, 2010, pitcher Armando Galarraga of the Detroit Tigers needed one more out in the ninth inning to finish a perfect game. When Cleveland's Jason Donald hit a grounder to Miguel Cabrera, Galarraga hustled to first to cover the bag. It was a close call, but Galarraga caught Cabrera's throw and stepped on the bag just ahead of the runner.

Time to celebrate, right? Nope.

Jim Joyce, the umpire, ruled Donald safe. Replays clearly showed that the umpire was wrong, but in 2010, overturning an umpire's ruling with replay wasn't yet a part of the rulebook. Galarraga kept calm, retiring the next batter. In the standings, Detroit chalked up another win, and Galarraga's pitching victory went down as a one-hit shutout. But the game stands as a great example of both the best and worst baseball has to offer. Galarraga pitched the best game of his life. Joyce made the worst call of his.

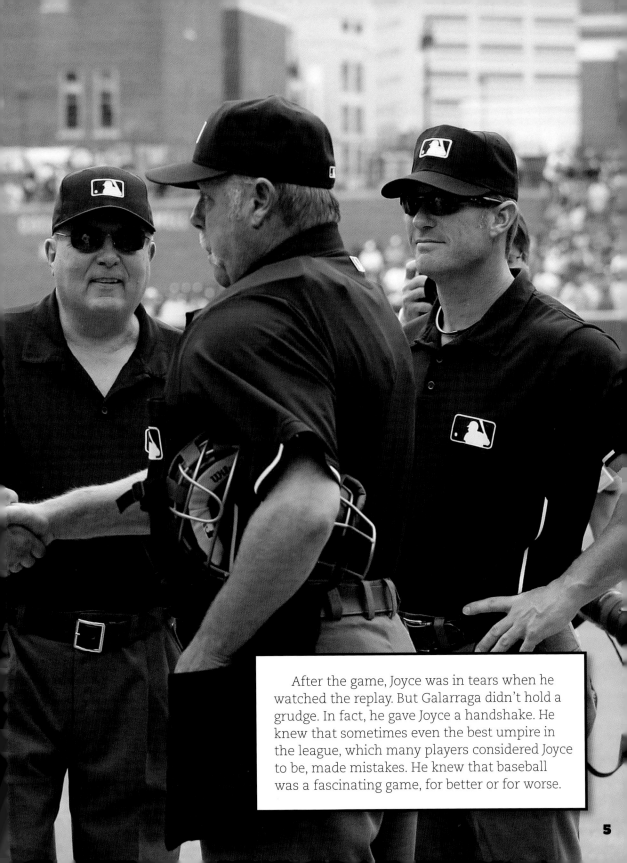

After the game, Joyce was in tears when he watched the replay. But Galarraga didn't hold a grudge. In fact, he gave Joyce a handshake. He knew that sometimes even the best umpire in the league, which many players considered Joyce to be, made mistakes. He knew that baseball was a fascinating game, for better or for worse.

# CHAPTER 1

# Offense & Defense

Babe Ruth

## BEST!

## HITTERS

It's the most compelling action in baseball: the bat hitting the ball. These batsmen, of course, come in all varieties. Some become legendary for their power, and some for their lack of skill.

Babe Ruth was a giant among boys on the baseball diamond. During his 22-year career, the "Sultan of Swat" smacked 714 home runs and posted a .342 batting average.

Legend has it the Babe once "called his own shot" during the 1932 World Series. The opposing Chicago Cubs were heckling Ruth from the dugout. Ruth was at the plate, down to his last strike. The Yankee great stared back. He pointed his bat to center field, as if to say, "Watch this, boys. I'm hitting it right over that wall." Sure enough, he crushed the next pitch into the center field seats.

The Babe retired like a boss, too. In the final week of his career, he hit three home runs in a single game.

## REMARKABLE ROOKIE

The Yankees found their latest All-Star slugger in 2017 when Aaron Judge took baseball by storm. The 25-year-old outfielder won the Home Run Derby during the All-Star break and bested Mark McGwire's major league record for home runs by a rookie by belting 52. During a July 22 game at Seattle's Safeco Field, Judge hit a home run so hard that statisticians couldn't estimate how far the ball traveled.

### FACT BREAK

Ted Williams hit .406 for the Boston Red Sox in 1941. Since then, no player has batted .400 or better. San Diego's Tony Gwynn was batting .394 in 1994 before a players' strike canceled the season in August, about 50 games shy of a full season.

Aaron Judge

# WORST!

There were batters with lower career batting averages than Mario Mendoza. But Mendoza lives in baseball infamy as the namesake of the "Mendoza Line."

**LIFE ON THE MENDOZA LINE**

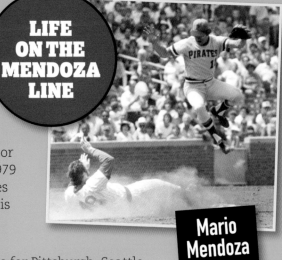

The Mendoza Line is a .200 batting average. Players batting below .200 are considered very poor hitters. The phrase was born in 1979 when Mendoza's Pittsburgh Pirates teammates teased him because his averaged hovered around .200.

But Mendoza was a stellar shortstop and played nine seasons for Pittsburgh, Seattle, and Texas. The Mexico native retired with an average (.215) above the Mendoza Line, and even batted .245 in 1980. Mendoza later became a minor league manager and was elected to the Mexican Baseball Hall of Fame.

Mario Mendoza

# PITCHERS

They are the hurlers of the ball. If they are on, the game flies by as fast as a backyard game of catch. When they're off, bats boom, baseballs fly over walls, and scoreboards light up.

## BEST!

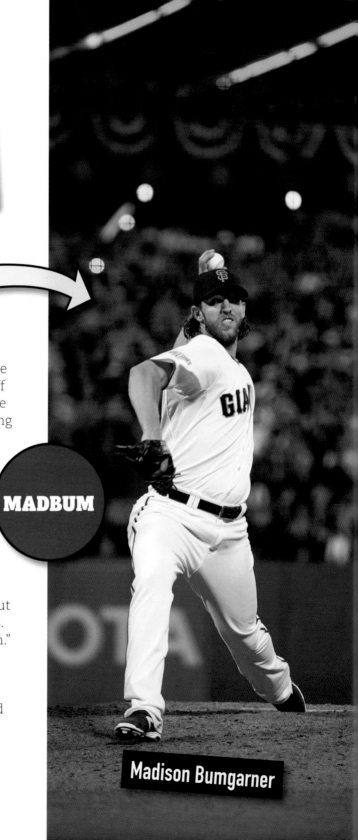

MADBUM

Madison Bumgarner

San Francisco's Madison Bumgarner became an instant legend during the 2014 playoffs. In the first two playoff rounds, the shaggy southpaw led the Giants to the World Series by pitching in the series-clinching games.

In Game 1 of the 2014 World Series, Bumgarner allowed one run across seven innings in a Giants win. Bumgarner notched another victory in Game 5 with a four-hit shutout. Then the 25-year-old saved his best for Game 7.

Most starting pitchers need about four days rest between appearances. Not the hurler nicknamed "MadBum." He pitched five innings of scoreless relief to preserve a one-run Giants victory to close out the series. For his efforts, Bumgarner earned World Series MVP and *Sports Illustrated* "Sportsman of the Year" honors.

Jake Arrieta

## QUALITY TIME

A pitcher has a "quality start" when he's pitched six or more innings and allowed three or fewer runs. From 2015 into 2016, Cubs pitcher Jake Arrieta pitched 24 consecutive quality starts, just two shy of Bob Gibson's record. The streak ended when Arrieta was pulled just one inning shy of another quality start.

# WORST!

Kansas City's Vin Mazzaro had a forgettable day at the ballpark in 2011. Unfortunately for Mazzaro, his pitching line is one baseball diehards won't forget.

With the Royals trailing the Cleveland Indians 3-0, Mazzaro came on in the third inning in relief of the starting pitcher and retired the side. Over the next two innings, however, the Indians clubbed in 14 runs at Mazzaro's expense. That's how Mazzaro became the first pitcher in modern MLB history to allow 14 runs in less than three innings. To his credit, Mazzaro rebounded after his worst game ever. He even went on to finish his career with a winning record of 24-23.

VIN MAZZARO'S NO GOOD, VERY BAD DAY

Vin Mazzaro

# FIELDERS

A well-turned double play or diving catch in the outfield rivals any monster home run or blazing strikeout. Likewise, poor fielding can make the newsreels — for all the wrong reasons.

## BEST!

## THE SAY HEY KID'S NO-WAY CATCH

The scene: a tie game in the eighth inning of Game 1 of the 1954 World Series. Cleveland's Vic Wertz hit a fly ball to deep center in the Polo Grounds. Willie Mays, the New York Giants star center fielder, raced to retrieve the ball, his back turned from home plate. Most fans assumed that Wertz's blast was going for extra bases.

But when Mays reached the warning track, he stretched out his glove. The ball flew over his shoulder and landed in his mitt like it had been magnetized there. The "Say Hey Kid" turned around and threw the ball into the infield as his hat fell to the ground.

Fans couldn't believe it. The Giants won the game and, eventually, the series.

Willie Mays

Jose Canseco was one of baseball's biggest sluggers during the 1980s and early 1990s. Fielding, however, was not his strong suit. Once during an early season game in 1993, Canseco was playing right field for the Texas Rangers. He lumbered after a high fly ball hit to the warning track. Turning his back to the wall, Canseco camped out under the ball and stuck out his glove. But the ball missed Canseco's glove, bounced off his head and . . . went over the fence for a home run!

Canseco rubbed his noggin, appearing amused. The slugger later joked the scorekeeper should've ruled the play a four-base error, not a home run.

# WORST!

## THAT'S USING YOUR HEAD!

Jose Canseco

Buster Posey

### FACTS AND STATS

San Francisco Giants catcher Buster Posey's career highlights fill a trophy room: three World Series titles, MVP and Rookie of the Year awards, and five All-Star selections. In 2016 Posey added a Gold Glove award to his collection.

# CHAPTER 2

# Champs & Choke Artists

No lead is ever safe in baseball. With nine full innings to complete, teams can't simply run out the clock. Put your rally caps on!

## BEST!

### REMARKABLE RED SOX RALLY

David Ortiz

The **New York Yankees** were once again beating up on their archrivals, the Boston Red Sox. The Yankees held a 3-0 series lead over the Sox in the 2004 American League Championship Series. Boston fans had seen this movie before. The ending never changed. The Yankees always won. But this year the "Curse of the Bambino" concluded with a twist.

The Sox won Games 4 and 5 in Boston behind slugger David Ortiz's heroics. The Sox then won Game 6 in New York, evening the series behind the pitching of Curt Schilling, who wore a — you can't make this up — bloody red sock.

Johnny Damon's Game 7 grand slam propelled Boston to the World Series, and the Sox shocked the Yankees by completing baseball's first 3-0 series comeback.

The Texas Rangers were one strike from their first World Series title. Twice. Both times, their leads disappeared.

In the 2011 World Series, Texas had a 3-2 series lead over the **St. Louis Cardinals**. In Game 6 the Rangers led 7–5 with two outs in the bottom of the ninth. Texas pitcher Neftali Feliz worked Cardinals third baseman David Freese to a 1–2 count.

TEXAS-SIZED MELTDOWN

WORST!

One more strike and Texas fans could rejoice!

The next pitch came in, and Freese smashed the ball to right field. Though the drive was deep, it was catchable. But Rangers right fielder Nelson Cruz misjudged the ball, allowing it to drop, and two runs scored to tie the game.

The Rangers scored two more runs and clung to another lead in the tenth inning. This time, Cardinals outfielder Lance Berkman, also down to his final strike, drove in two runs. The Cardinals later won Game 6 on a Freese home run and were victorious in Game 7.

CURSES!!!

**FACTS AND STATS**
In 2011 the Red Sox suffered their own historic collapse. That season, Boston became the first team to fail to reach the playoffs after holding a nine-game division lead in September.

13

**CUBS WIN!
CUBS WIN!
CUBS WIN!**

# LEGENDS

October baseball is edge-of-your-seat excitement. The do-or-die nature of the games can bring cheers or agony. Some matchups exceed expectations. Others don't live up to the hype.

By the end of the 2016 World Series, many observers wished neither team had to lose. But there are no ties in baseball.

The **Chicago Cubs** hadn't won a World Series in so long (108 years) they were dubbed the "lovable losers." The **Cleveland Indians** had been stuck in a title drought since 1948.

The Cubs battled back from a three-games-to-one hole to force a Game 7 in Cleveland. One team's fan base was going to be ecstatic. Another legion of fans would be devastated.

Chicago built a 6–3 lead going into the bottom of the eighth inning. Though it was clear that the Indians would not go down easily, Cubs fans could taste victory. Chicago was six outs away from becoming champs.

Cleveland started a two-out rally in the eighth. Two straight hits produced a run, and then light-hitting second baseman Rajai Davis stepped to the plate. Davis stunned the baseball world when he lunged at Aroldis Chapman's offering and pulled a screaming liner just over the left field wall at Progressive Field. Pandemonium hit Cleveland.

The game was tied!

Cubs fans buried their heads in their hands in despair. In the blink of an eye, their dream-come-true ending was turning into a nightmare. Then things really got weird.

After a scoreless ninth inning, clouds over Cleveland began to pour rain. Both teams went back to their clubhouses as the umpires halted play. After a 17-minute rain delay, the tenth inning got underway.

In the top of the tenth, the Cubs scored twice to take an 8-6 lead. But the Indians scored with two outs to close the gap to 8-7. Cleveland outfielder Michael Martinez strolled to the plate, representing the World Series-winning run. The entire season came down to one at-bat.

Rajai Davis

The Cubs brought in reliever Michael Montgomery, who threw a curveball for strike one. Montgomery's second pitch, another curve, forced Martinez to hit a dribbler. Cubs third baseman Kris Bryant fielded the ball and grinned like a Little Leaguer as he threw to first. Anthony Rizzo caught the final out, and Cubs nation celebrated. It was a game for the ages.

Chicago World Series celebration

**FACT BREAK**
When the Cubs held their victory parade following the 2016 World Series, Chicago went wild. Approximately 5 million people attended, making it the seventh-largest gathering in human history.

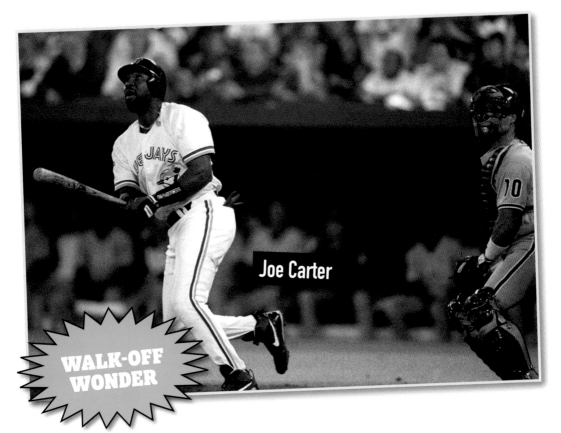

Joe Carter

**WALK-OFF WONDER**

The World Series has ended on a walk-off home run only twice. In 1960 Bill Mazeroski of the Pittsburgh Pirates hit a Game 7 home run to defeat the Yankees. The 1993 Toronto Blue Jays also pulled off a World Series Walk-Off when Joe Carter launched a rocket into the left field seats of Game 6 in Toronto against the Phildelphia Phillies. Carter was so excited after his homer that he could barely make it around the bases as he skipped, jumped, and shouted with joy.

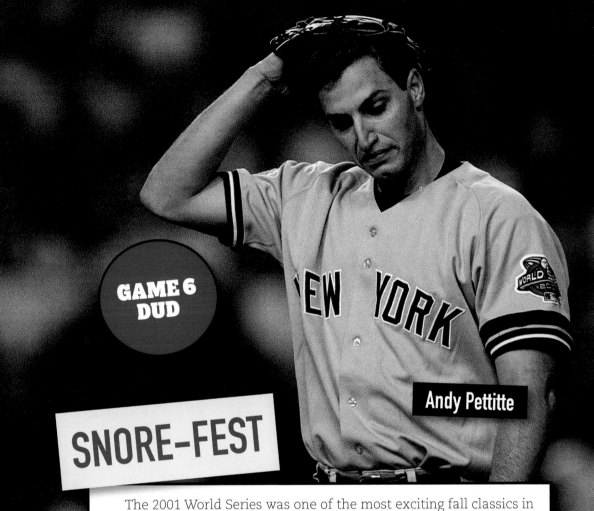

GAME 6
DUD

Andy Pettitte

## SNORE-FEST

The 2001 World Series was one of the most exciting fall classics in MLB history. The Series featured two walk-off wins, the league's first game that went into the month of November, and a championship capped by a thrilling Game 7. Game 6, however, was a total blowout, and one of the biggest snoozers in World Series history.

The Series returned to Arizona with the New York Yankees a win away from their 28th World Series title. Any hopes the Yanks had of winning Game 6 quickly evaporated. The **Diamondbacks** scored a run in the first inning, three in the second to chase Yankee pitcher Andy Pettitte, eight in the third, and another three in the fourth. Down 15-0 going into the top of the fifth inning, you couldn't blame the Yankees if they gave up. Especially with Diamondbacks ace pitcher Randy Johnson on the mound.

The Yankees finally scored a pair of runs in the sixth inning to avoid being shut out. But by the time the game was over, the D-backs finished with six doubles and a World Series-record 22 hits.

# CHAPTER 3

# Fun & Fashion

## MASCOTS

BEST OF THE JEST

Let's face it: Baseball can get a little S-L-O-W. Thankfully there are mascots to liven things up.

During every home game in the nation's capital, mascots modeled after six former presidents in Washington Nationals uniforms race around the field. The President's Race has spawned a legion of fans. Poor Teddy Roosevelt, a fan favorite, ran for nearly seven years before he won his first race! He still has a long way to go to beat current all-time race winner, Abraham Lincoln.

**Orbit Astro** pulled a fast one on Los Angeles Angels star Mike Trout. Before a game in April 2017, Astro waddled up to Trout and put his arm around the slugger. Trout didn't notice Orbit had slapped a piece of paper that read, "I love the Astros" on the back of Trout's jersey. Even the best players in baseball can fall victim to a mascot prank.

# BEST!

The Phillie Phanatic is arguably the goofiest mascot in baseball. There are few stunts the Phanatic is unwilling to try, be it taunting the opposing teams or dancing on the tops of dugouts. In 2010 the Phanatic put on dancing shoes and impersonated Lady Gaga.

**Bernie Brewer** and his mustache are such a fixture at Milwaukee Brewers home games that the foam-headed mascot has his own dugout in the left field bleachers. After every home run at Miller Park, Bernie glides down a yellow slide onto a platform in the shape of home plate.

## WORST OF THE QUIRKS

Mariner Moose had reason to celebrate in 1995 when the Seattle Mariners reached the American League Divisional Series. During Game 4, the Moose was riding behind an ATV on a pair of roller blades. As the ATV took a sharp turn, the Moose let go of the rope. Mariner Moose began flailing his arms and crashed full-speed into the wall. The result was a season-ending broken ankle. Ouch!

In 1984 the San Francisco Giants picked a mascot that the fans were supposed to dislike. The Giants' plan worked as fans pelted **Crazy Crab** with batteries and bottles. Crazy Crab was retired after one season, but the Crab returned for one game in 1999. Now there's a Crazy Crab sandwich at the Giants' ballpark.

## FACT BREAK

In a 1999 game, longtime Dodgers manager Tommy Lasorda wasn't amused by the antics of **Youppi!**, a Montreal Expos mascot. Lasorda complained to umpires about Youppi!'s unsportsmanlike behavior, and the mascot was ejected from the game. The Expos, minus their mascot, went on to lose, 1–0, in 22 innings.

# HAIR

Some baseball players like to stand out in a crowd. Some prefer to let their hair down, while others appear allergic to razors. A select few fall victim to haircut hilarity.

## BEST!

**LET IT GROW**

Brian Wilson

Brian Wilson began growing his bushy black beard during San Francisco's 2010 pennant chase. The beard grew its own slogan: Fear the Beard. Wilson didn't shave the beard again until his comeback attempt in 2017.

Baseball players just don't grow mustaches anymore like Rollie Fingers, who played from 1968 to 1985, did. The relief pitcher's handlebar 'stache remains the gold standard for above-the-lip coolness. Kids, don't try this at home.

**Coco Crisp** wasn't afraid to try bold hairdos. The center fielder favored cornrows and a huge afro that grew so large that he had difficulty wearing a hat or helmet. Crisp even experimented with a fade on the top and grew a sort of "mustache" on the back of his neck. Let's give Crisp an E for effort.

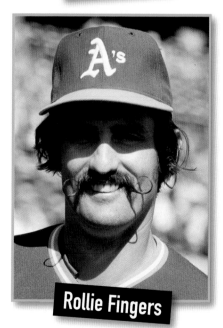

Rollie Fingers

Lanky left-handed hurler **Randy Johnson** was a towering figure on the pitcher's mound for an amazing 22 MLB seasons from 1988 to 2009. But his long, curly mullet was a fashion strikeout.

Everyone loved John Kruk for his down-home wit. His 1993 Phillies team sported a lot of funky hair, but Kruk's thick mullet and facial hair stood out among the group's so-called club, "Macho Row."

Washington Nationals phenom **Bryce Harper** might well end up in the Hall of Fame. But his Mohawk and evolving bushy hairstyles bring him attention that's not always so positive.

WORST!

CUT IT OUT!

John Kruk

## SHAVE IT OR LEAVE IT
The New York Yankees have no tolerance for long hair or beards, though mustaches are allowed. In 1986 Yankees star first baseman Don Mattingly ignored the ban and let his hair grow shaggy. The team called his bluff and removed him from the lineup and fined him $250. Mattingly promptly got a haircut. When Mattingly was named manager of the Miami Marlins, he banned all of his players from sporting facial hair. He reversed the policy in 2017.

# UNIFORMS

Over the course of the season, fans become very familiar with each team's uniforms. Some are memorable, but others we wish we'd never see again.

**BEST-DRESSED**

The Chicago Cubs' bear logo is one of baseball's best. The deep blue against the red and white has that touch of Americana that is pleasing to the eyes.

**BEST!**

When you've won as many World Series as the Yankees (27), classic pinstripes never go out of style. Their home jerseys don't feature players' names on the back, a rarity in baseball.

The Oakland Athletics have always taken risks with their green and yellow jerseys. It can be a good move to stand out when surrounded by the crowd.

The **White Sox** retro black-and-white uniforms, which they brought back in the 1990s, should be here to stay.

The Cardinals don't reinvent the wheel with their uniforms, which have undergone only minor tweaks. With baseball jerseys, "simple" sparkles.

BEST!

## FACTS AND STATS

In the early days of Major League Baseball, players didn't wear numbers on the jerseys. It wasn't until 1929 that a game featured both teams with numbered uniforms.

# WORST!

**FASHION FAILS!**

The Houston Astros 1970s uniforms were an eyesore. Red, orange, and yellow don't belong together on a uniform. And numbers look better on jerseys than pantlegs.

During the cut-off sleeve phase of the late 1990s and the early 2000s, the Arizona Diamondbacks tried a pinstripe cut-off with a purple T-shirt. When done right, cut-off jerseys look sharp. Arizona's was a ghastly sight.

There's a reason no other team went for a teal jersey color until the **Florida Marlins** tried in the 1990s.

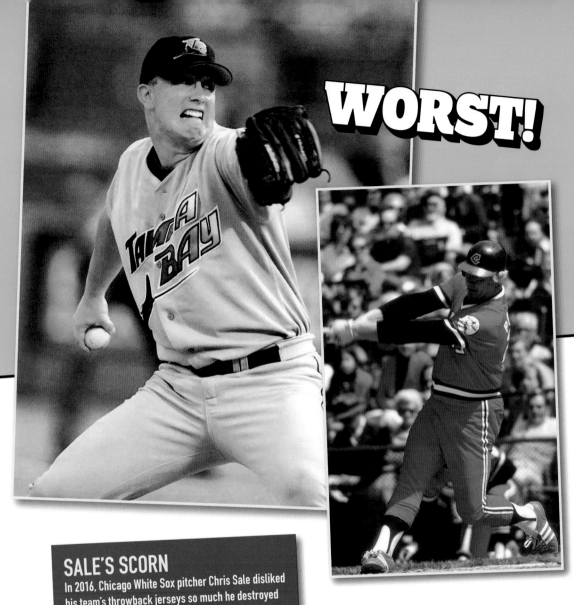

# WORST!

## SALE'S SCORN

In 2016, Chicago White Sox pitcher Chris Sale disliked his team's throwback jerseys so much he destroyed them with a pair of scissors. Sale was fined by the team for the cost of the jerseys — $12,700 — and suspended him for five games.

The Tampa Bay Devil Rays' original rainbow-colored logo was a strange look. The team won't wear their original uniforms when they have "throwback jersey" nights.

The Cleveland Indians' 1975 road uniforms sported red jerseys and red pants. The players looked like tomatoes — yuck! The Indians realized their fashion mistake and restyled the uniforms after only three years.

# CHAPTER 4

# Rules & Reflections

## UNWRITTEN RULES

There are many rules in the game of baseball. And then there are the goofy unwritten rules. When hit by a pitch, don't rub it. Don't admire your home run. Don't steal a base if you're way ahead. Don't bunt to break up a no-hitter. If a pitcher beans your teammate, you should bean one of his. Baseball works in mysterious ways.

**SHHHH!**

Ballplayers learn early in their careers that if a pitcher is midway through the game and still hasn't allowed a hit, they better not utter a word in the dugout about the matter, especially to the pitcher.

Why not?

You could jinx the pitcher! Actually, don't even think about sitting next to the pitcher during a no-hitter. Stay far away and keep quiet. Loose lips sink ships.

In pro baseball, the object of the game is to score more runs than the opponent for the full nine innings. Pretty simple, right? But at some point, an unwritten rule was created: When a team is winning by a wide margin, it's not OK for a batter to swing when the count is 3-0.

Those who believe in the rule will argue that trying to "run up the score" is disrespectful to the opposition. But who makes these silly rules, anyway? If a rule is unwritten, it's pretty difficult to know if it's being broken

LOOK OUT!

## FACTS AND STATS

In 2017 the Miami Marlins were furious when a Los Angeles Dodgers batter swung at a 3-0 pitch with the Marlins trailing 5-0 in the seventh. Hitters from both teams were beaned by pitches. A benches-clearing brawl ensued. It wasn't the first time.

# QUOTES

Baseball players and managers can say the strangest things when a microphone is thrust in their faces every day. Their responses can be hilarious, infuriating, or profound.

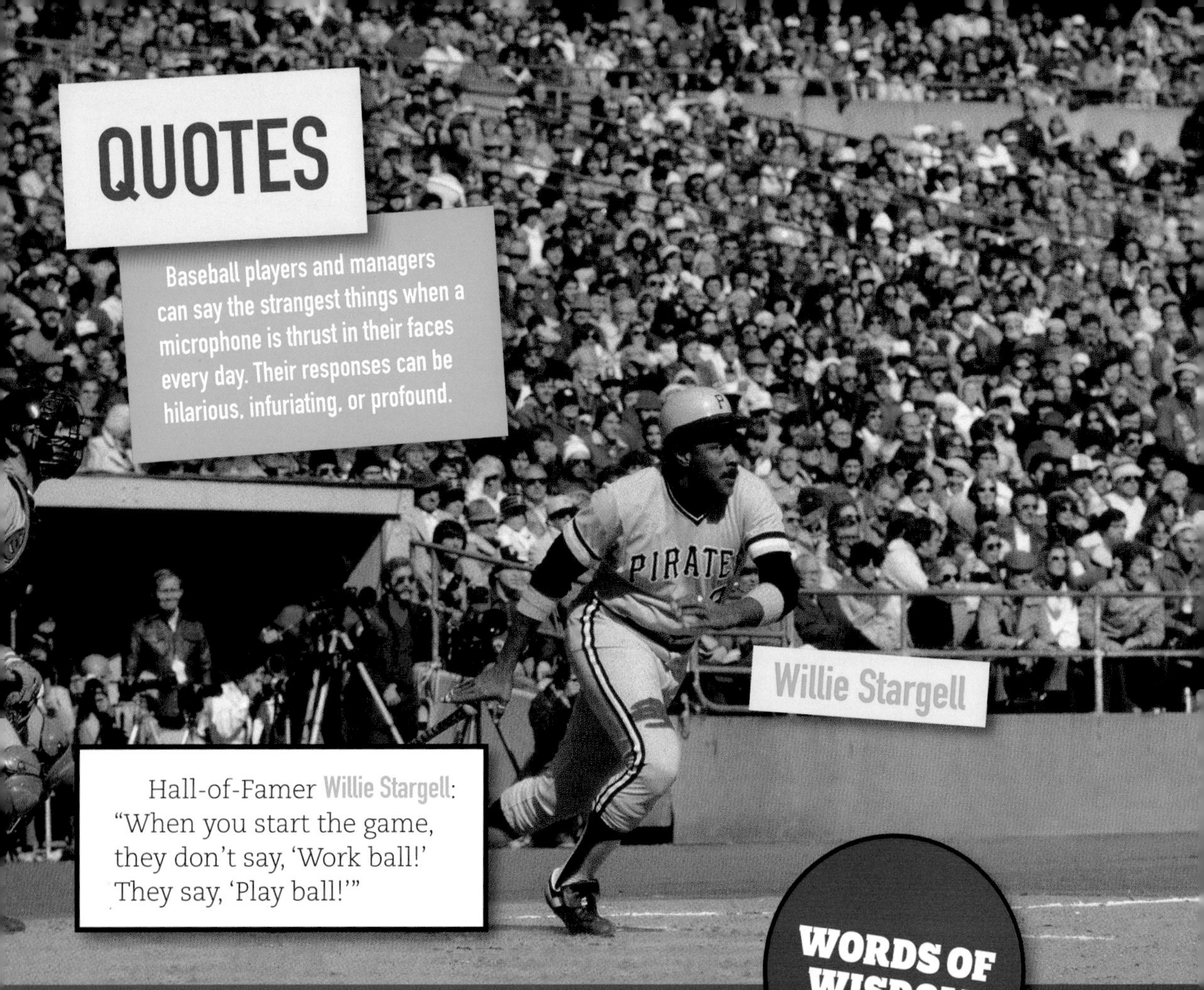

Willie Stargell

Hall-of-Famer Willie Stargell: "When you start the game, they don't say, 'Work ball!' They say, 'Play ball!'"

## WORDS OF WISDOM

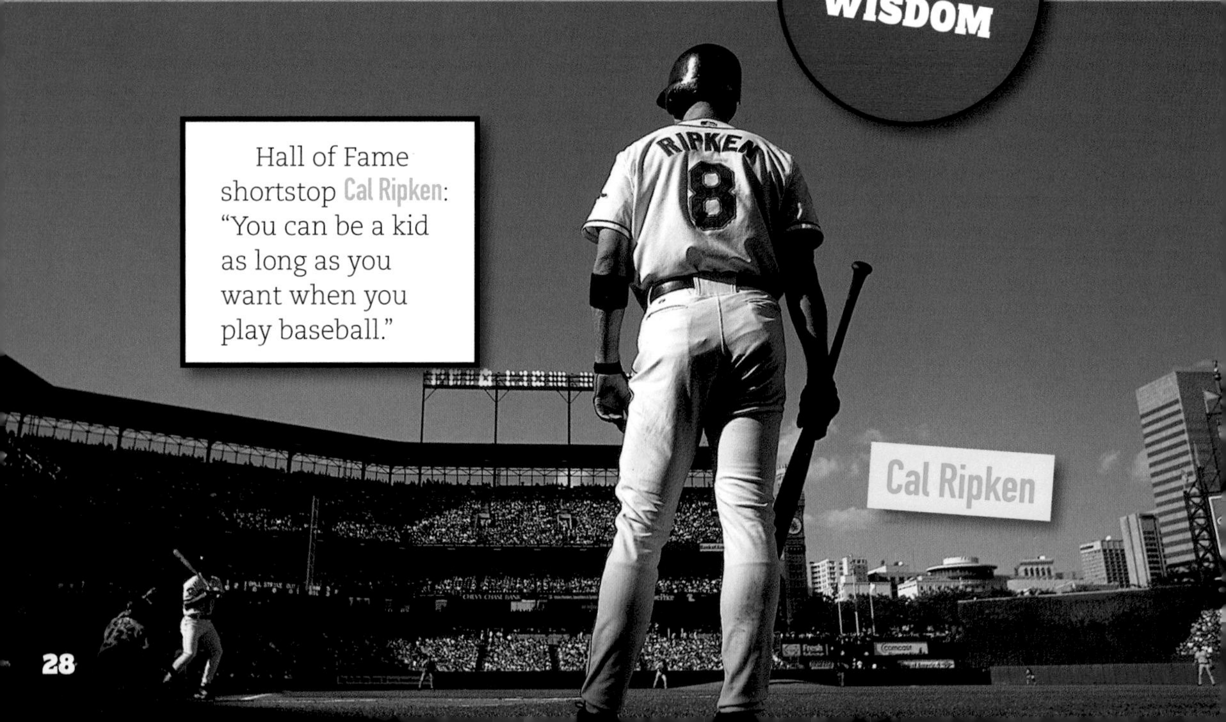

Hall of Fame shortstop Cal Ripken: "You can be a kid as long as you want when you play baseball."

Cal Ripken

Dan Quisenberry

Pitcher Dan Quisenberry: "The best thing about baseball is there's no homework."

Former All-Star **John Kruk**: "I'm not an athlete. I'm a professional baseball player."

Yogi Berra

SAY WHAT?

Hall of Fame catcher Yogi Berra: "Baseball is 90 percent mental. The other half is physical."

Dizzy Dean

Baltimore Orioles manager **Buck Showalter**: "That's one great thing about this game — you don't have to shave every day."

Hall-of-Famer **Phil Rizzuto**: "I'm glad I don't play anymore. I couldn't learn all of those handshakes."

Hall of Fame pitcher Dizzy Dean, after a 1-0 game: "The game was closer than the score indicated."

The *Cincinnati Gazette* newspaper, 1879: "This baseball mania has run its course. It has no future as a professional endeavor."

# ABOUT THE AUTHOR

Drew Lyon's first magazine subscription was *Sports Illustrated for Kids*. He soon developed a lifelong love of reading and writing. He has been a freelance writer for more than 10 years and specializes in sports and culture pieces. He currently writes for *Minnesota Soybean Business Magazine*. Drew lives in Mankato, Minnesota, where he can often be found devouring biographies and crime novels.

# GLOSSARY

**bean** — to hit someone with a pitch

**fall classic** — a nickname for the World Series; refers to the fact that the World Series is always played following the summer, in the fall

**heckle** — to interrupt (someone, such as a speaker or performer) by shouting annoying or rude comments or questions

**namesake** — someone or something that has the same name as another person or thing

**no-hitter** — a game in which a pitcher does not allow the batters from the other team to get a base hit

**perfect game** — a game in which all the batters from one team are retired in order, with no one reaching base

**pinstripes** — thin, vertical stripes on cloth

**rival** — a person or thing that tries to defeat or be more successful than another

**rule book** — a book that contains the official set of rules that must be followed in a game

**shutout** — a game or contest in which one side does not score

**southpaw** — someone who is left-handed

**umpire** — a person who controls play and makes sure that players act according to the rules in a sports event

# READ MORE

**Braun, Eric.** *Know the Stats: Baseball.* North Mankato, Minn.: Capstone, 2017.

**The Editors of Sports Illustrated for Kids.** *Baseball: Then to Wow!* Sports Illustrated. 2016.

**Omoth, Tyler.** *Six Degrees of David Ortiz: Connecting Baseball Stars.* North Mankato, Minn.: Capstone, 2015.

# INTERNET SITES

Use FactHound to find Internet sites related to this book.

Visit *www.facthound.com*

Just type in 9781543506136 and go.

# INDEX